Alcoholics Redeemed

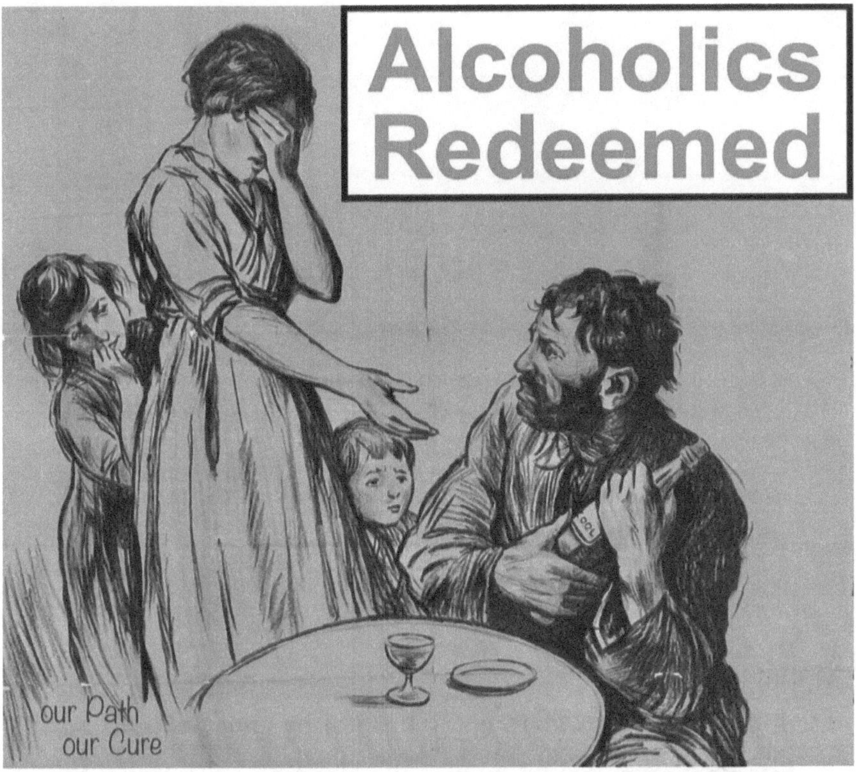

AR

HOPE * HEALING * RECOVERY

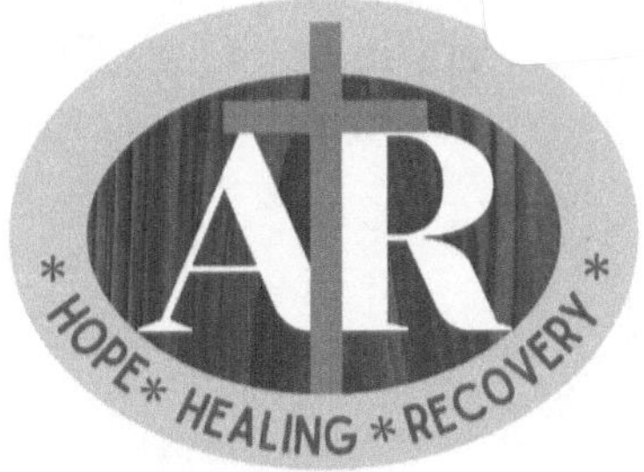

ISBN 979-8-89112-819-4 (Paperback)
ISBN 979-8-89112-820-0 (Digital)

Covenant Books
11661 Hwy 707
Murrells Inlet, SC 29576
www.covenantbooks.com

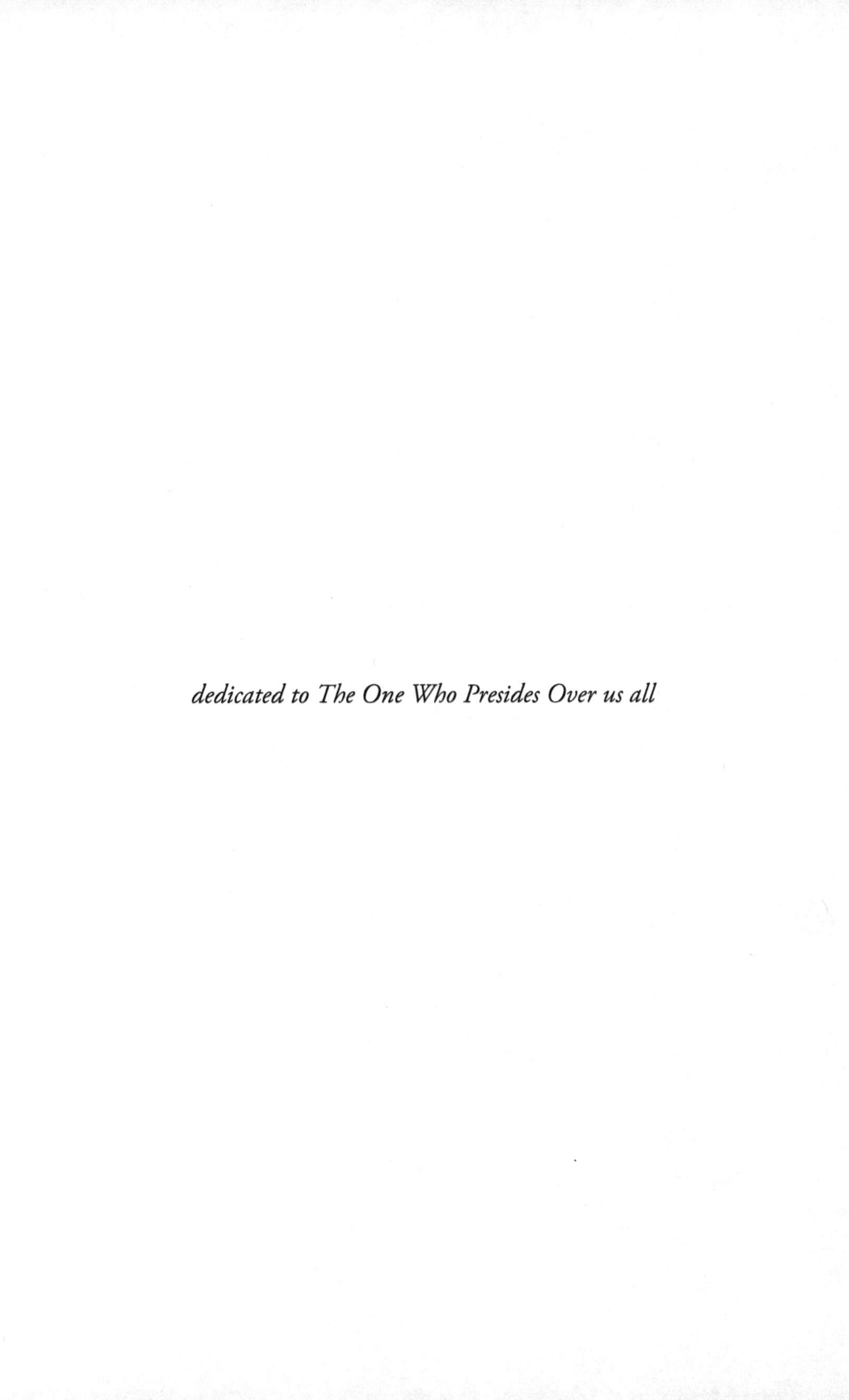

dedicated to The One Who Presides Over us all

CONTENTS

CHAPTER 1

About Alcoholism

A drunkard is a sinner; however, alcoholism is a disease. Most people hear the word disease, and their imagination automatically runs wild. They think of rashes, bumps, and all kinds of deformities. We of Alcoholics Redeemed believe there is a big misunderstanding of what this alcoholic illness really is. A simple definition of *disease* is an illness or sickness characterized by specific signs and symptoms. And when it comes to alcoholism, the signs and symptoms are an obsession to drink that takes place in our mind, followed by a physical craving for another drink that takes place in our body. This physical craving is caused by the drink itself and results in a compulsion to continuously consume more alcohol.

Back in the 1930s, a well-known doctor named William D. Silkworth specialized in the treatment of alcoholism. He described this physical craving as an allergy to alcohol. Dr. Silkworth stated that anyone suffering from alcoholic torture must believe that the body of an alcoholic is quite as abnormal as his/her mind. This confirms why we alcoholics have absolutely no control over our drinking once we take any alcohol into our system. This explains why we were always watching the clock, making sure we could make it to the liquor store before closing, even after leaving the bar. We were always thinking about how much alcohol we had left to determine if we could make it through the day. Some of us were even afraid to go on family vacations or events, knowing that we couldn't drink the way we wanted to or that there wouldn't be enough to drink when we got there. Therefore, we believe that a complete picture of an alcoholic must include both physical and mental factors.

Once an alcoholic takes any alcohol into his system, it triggers the allergy, and the body demands another drink, making it almost impossible to stop once we start. We make promises over and over again to quit and sincerely mean it, but then something happens in our mind, and we cave in every time, repeating this cycle over and over again. Unfortunately, this illness can only be diagnosed by the individuals themselves. People around us, such as our family and coworkers, see our problem. Their solution is to say things like "grow up," "stop destroying your life," "quit drinking and get your act together," or "make better decisions." They no more understand the problem than we do. As for us and our twisted thinking, we'll say things like "you would drink too if you had him or her," or "if you had a rough childhood," or "if you were in the military" and so on. However, if we really get honest with ourselves, we really don't know why we drink. If we did, we wouldn't go to the extremes we do concerning alcohol. We wouldn't lose jobs, lose families, and sad to say, even drink ourselves to death.

The first step in solving a problem is to diagnose the problem first. We have to get honest with ourselves: Can I control my drinking? Can I stop when I want to? Are there consequences when I drink? Do I get more pain than pleasure when I drink? Don't get us wrong, we of Alcoholics Redeemed have had lots of pleasure at one time from drinking. That's why we were obsessed with it in the first place. It did miraculous things for us. One of our members described the feeling he got from drinking as when Popeye ate his spinach. Another member described this feeling as, "Calgon, take me away." It gave us a great feeling of ease and comfort, taking away all our insecurities. However, as time went on, this illness progressed and seemed to turn on us, and our problems got worse. And when our problems got worse, our drinking increased.

One of our members once had his children taken from him. His answer was to go to the bar and try to solve his problem. In his insanity, he couldn't see that the reason he lost his children in the first place was because of his drinking problem. His answer was a drink, and it became more of a problem. Therefore, the answer became the problem, and the problem became the answer.

Now we may sound like a broken record, but isn't this the story of our lives? Each of us kept doing the same thing over and over again. There was always one more attempt to quit and one more failure, then waking up with deep remorse. We had to drink even when we didn't want to drink. Life became too hard to handle sober, but to drink meant alcoholic torture. So many alcoholics have taken their own lives. So many wish they could, all the while never knowing what's wrong with themselves.

In summary, alcoholism is an obsession in our mind, preoccupying us with thoughts and ideas about drinking. This leads to the insanity of that first drink, setting off an allergic reaction that creates a thirst for more alcohol, and we are unable to control it. This inability to control our drinking eventually leads to blackouts, passing out, drunk tanks, treatment centers, and sad to say, even death. However, cheer up. There is hope, a great hope!

CHAPTER 2

Redemption

There is no greater gift than God's redeeming love. This is the message that we hope will touch those who still suffer.

No words can describe the utter despair, loneliness, and hopelessness we felt in those final days of drinking. We were at that jump-off place. We couldn't imagine life anymore with or without alcohol. Our world was upside-down. Our relationships were in turmoil. Our finances were shot. We had been kicked, damned, disgusted with, fired, rehired, and refired. Life became impossible. We had hit the bottom of all bottoms. But for the grace of God, there could have been even worse tragedies. Finding ourselves at this junction in the road, we had but three alternatives: drink, die, or find a better way.

We of Alcoholics Redeemed have found a better way that really works. We have the freedom to go anywhere without the fear of picking up a drink. Where we used to cringe going into certain stores or seeing advertisements and commercials, we now have peace, joy, and contentment. Our families and friendships have been restored. We have gained respect in our homes and in our communities.

Our simple program is designed to give you a vital *life-changing* experience, which will not only conquer your alcoholism but also give you a way of living that will answer all your problems. This is a great fact for us! Each of us now knows that we are part of a divine miracle. This you can know too! It was only a matter of admitting complete defeat, setting aside any prejudice, getting honest with ourselves, and facing our own mistakes. With this attitude, you cannot fail. Our hope is that the reader will find the peace and purpose that we have found in this simple path of living.

In the back of this book, you will read some of our personal testimonies. Each individual gives an account of the miracle that actually took place in his/her life. We hope that you identify with some and gain confidence to go forward and join us in this fellowship of the redeemed.

CHAPTER 3

Our Path, Our Cure

Alcoholics Redeemed is a fellowship of men, women, family, and friends who have once suffered or know someone suffering from alcoholism. To show others how we got out from under is the main purpose of our movement. Many do not understand that the true alcoholic is a very sick person. And besides, we are sure that our way of living has its advantages for all.

Our stories testify to what our lives used to be like, the miracle that took place, and how wonderful our lives are now. If you have decided you want what we have and are willing to sacrifice anything to get it, then perhaps you are ready to follow directions. Remember, we are dealing with a deadly illness, and without God's divine help, we are doomed. So trust in the Lord with all your heart, and lean not on your own understanding. Draw near to Him, and He shall draw near to you.

Here is our path to redemption:

1. We were completely defeated, realizing we were hopeless apart from divine help.
2. We surrendered ourselves entirely to God.
3. We confessed our sins and humbly asked God to cleanse us through His Son, Jesus Christ.
4. We made restitution for harms done to others.

5. We commune daily with God and seek guidance from Him through His spirit.
6. We meet and fellowship regularly with other believers.
7. We witness and share our testimonies with others, especially alcoholics, and practice love and service in all areas of our lives.

Now this may seem like a tall order; however, pain is a great motivator. None of us were capable of handling anything hard when we got here. We were already overwhelmed, and we needed something simple, and this program is simple. When the pain of the problem became worse than the pain of the solution, we were open and grateful to accept.

If you are completely defeated and convinced you will never beat the game on your own strength, it's time to get completely honest with yourself.

Can you truly see that you have an illness, which is incurable from a medical viewpoint? Do you honestly want to quit drinking forever? Are you willing to sacrifice anything to make this possible? If you have answered yes to these questions without any reservation, congratulations, you have taken the first step toward victory.

To be doomed to an alcoholic hell or be saved are not always easy alternatives to face. However, they are the only choices for a true alcoholic of our type. If you have arrived at this point of surrender, congratulations! Not many get this opportunity. Desperation is a gift, and we are all fortunate to have gotten here.

Although our willpower was strong in some areas, probably too strong to say the least, it was not sufficient enough to keep us from the insanity of that first drink. Therefore, we were willing to give up on our will and accept God's will. For this act of surrender to be concrete, we must believe that God is and will! This decision requires an act of faith, and we of AR can tell you, it has been the best decision we have ever made.

When ready, get down on your knees if possible. God knows what's truly in your heart. Humbly offer yourself as a living sacrifice to Him by saying this prayer:

> God, take me as a piece of clay and mold me
> into what You would have me be.

Congratulations on your commitment; however, we must go further. As fishermen, we know that you can't clean fish before you catch 'em. You catch 'em then clean 'em. It's just like this when we have sin in us that separates us from God. Sin is like a barrier that blocks us off from God. Sin is so serious, and God loved us so much that He sent His one and only begotten Son to die for it. This should bring about real humility to admit our faults, confess them, and have God remove them.

We don't have the power to remove them on our own. The blood of Christ makes this possible! Here are some examples of what we need to admit and confess:

- Resentment, anger, hate __________________________
- Fear, cowardice __________________________
- Self-pity __________________________
- Self-justification __________________________
- Self-importance, egotism, idolatry __________________________
- Self-condemnation, shame __________________________
- Lying, evasiveness, dishonesty __________________________
- Impatience __________________________
- False pride, phoniness, denial __________________________
- Jealousy, envy __________________________
- Laziness, procrastination __________________________
- Insincerity __________________________
- Negative thinking __________________________
- Immoral thinking, lust, adultery __________________________
- Perfectionism, intolerance __________________________
- Criticizing, loose talk, gossip __________________________
- Greed __________________________

We get honest with ourselves about which ones we have, placing a check mark by each one. Not everyone has all of these, yet most of us had about ten to fifteen. However, one is too many! God says, if we broke one, we have broken them all.

Next, we find an understanding person, a fellow believer, to share this with. After all, God promised to be in the midst where two or three are gathered together in His name. These shortcomings are best talked through with another person. It is so easy to deceive ourselves and escape the real humiliation of sin and evade the necessary action to bring about a life change to recover from alcoholism.

After this humbling experience, we go to a quiet place, thanking God for what He has done for us. We pause for a few minutes, going over our list again, making sure we left nothing out. If we happen to feel guilty at this point, it's a good thing. It brings about real conviction when we finally see our part in all this.

When ready, we get back down on our knees again. Approaching our Maker in a humble manner, admitting we are nothing without Him, we say, "Dear Heavenly Father, I know that I'm a sinner, and I ask for Your forgiveness. I believe Jesus died for my sins and rose from the dead. I repent of my sins. I invite You to come into my heart and life. I want to trust and follow You as my Lord and Savior. May I do Your will always. In Jesus's name, amen."

God has forgiven us. He doesn't want to hear about our past anymore. He himself said, "It is finished." He has washed our slate clean. We are now under His grace. The freedom from guilt and shame is priceless!

CHAPTER 4

First Things First

By now, we hope you can see that this is a life-changing program. As this miracle of healing begins to take place, we will at times feel safe and protected. However, we must be willing to go further, for faith without works is dead!

Therefore, we begin making our restitution. Start out by making a list of names of people we have harmed, whether it be verbally, physically, emotionally, or financially. Also, include those whom we have felt deep resentment toward.

Some of these people should not be approached, for it would cause more harm. So we pray for them and leave that up to God for now. Some people may have passed on, and we leave that up to God also. He knows what we are able to do and not do. However, we must make an honest attempt to approach the ones we can and try to amend what's broken. The attitude of willingness to do this is what's important. If we have this willingness to right our wrongs, God makes it possible!

People We Harmed	Who We Resented	Who We Owe Money
_______________	_______________	_______________
_______________	_______________	_______________
_______________	_______________	_______________
_______________	_______________	_______________

Start out by doing the ones that are easier and close by. Most people will gladly accept and wish us well. Keep in mind though that we should have no expectations of the outcome. Our sole purpose is to own our part. Don't be surprised if you happen to run into someone on your list out of the blue. Many of us have experienced this. God is truly in control when we let Him. He will often put people in our path.

Some people have heard us say sorry over and over again. This word has lost its meaning, especially to our families. In these cases, actions speak louder than words. For example, one member hadn't seen his children in years. Saying sorry wasn't going to cut it. However, he accepted the program outlined in this book, and his life changed dramatically. After fulfilling his obligations to the court, he was reunited with his children, and they saw the change in their dad.

They gladly accepted him, and today the whole family lives in peace and has a life filled with blessings that they never thought possible. This is another example of "God can and will" if we sincerely seek Him and live out a surrendered life.

Facing someone we have resented is probably the most difficult. But if we skip out on this, we may miss out on some of the best blessings this program has to offer. It may even lead to a future conversion. When we hand over our anger to God, He takes charge, and forgiveness begins to take shape. Someone we could not stand or ever feel like we could face, suddenly appears to us in a new light.

Love begins to take its place. Remember, we have the power of God with us, and He doesn't fail. God will never leave us or forsake us.

If there is one part of this phase of restitution that does take time, it's definitely our financial amends. Most of us owed money to family members, creditors, child support, back taxes, etc. But we don't dodge them. As we get back on our feet, we simply take them one at a time. We make honest phone calls, setting up payment plans. If we were smart enough to take it, we ought to be smart enough to pay it back. We simply cannot live in the present if we are still dragging around our past!

If we have carefully followed directions and made a sincere effort toward cleaning up our past, we will be amazed when we feel God's spirit come into us. We will have gone from a belief to actually having a life-changing experience with God. We will bear the fruits of His spirit. We will have joy, peace, patience, kindness, goodness, and self-control. We will experience real freedom from the bondage we used to be in. We are reborn!

> Therefore, if any man be in Christ, he is a
> new creature: old things are passed away; behold,
> all things are become new. (2 Corinthians 5:17
> KJV)

CHAPTER 5

Grace

Congratulations on your new life! We now know the real problem of the true alcoholic. We were separated from God all along. It's been said that *grace* stands for "God's riches at Christ's expense." By riches, we mean victory, forgiveness, peace, reconciliation, and redemption. For this we are deeply indebted to Him.

Now that we have been gifted the power that conquered our alcoholism, the next step is to continue building our relationship with God. This is the true meaning of "one day at a time," living in His presence, being aware of things that block us off from doing God's will. We practice this new way of living as we continue with our restitution.

When defects or sinful thoughts creep up, we ask God to remove them at once. This keeps us on the offense rather than being on defense, like we used to. It also keeps us from falling back into self-pity and having a negative attitude.

Thankfulness must go with us constantly. When we make mistakes or hurt someone, we make amends right away. Remember to ask God for His forgiveness. This keeps our slate clean. As we practice this new discipline, God will provide the power of temperance and restraint for the days ahead. Doing this daily keeps us in constant communion with God. He has a job and a purpose for our lives, so seek His will above all else. He will never put anything on our hearts that He doesn't give us the power to see it through! To experience God's love and love toward our fellow man is a feeling like no other. It brings about real service. We now work for God. How many get this privilege? Very few. But we believe it's here for all who honestly seek Him.

Below is a detailed outline of our daily plan for living:

Morning

- When we wake up, we thank God for another day.
- Ask God to direct our thinking and remove any selfish motives quickly.
- Read one or two verses out of the Bible, or use a devotional to read that includes Bible verses.
- Pause and listen for a few minutes.

Morning prayer: "God, direct my thinking today so that it be empty of self-pity, dishonesty, self-will, self-seeking, and fear. I ask You to inspire my thinking, decisions, and intuitions. Help me to relax and take it easy. Free me from doubt and indecisiveness. Guide me through this day, and show me my next step. God, show me what I need to do to take care of any problems. I ask these things that I may serve You to the fullest. Amen."

Throughout the day, watch for negative thinking, irritations, and fear. When we feel any of these, ask God to remove them at once.

- Pray for people or situations that we have ill feelings toward.
- If we hurt someone, we make amends quickly. Remember to ask God for forgiveness.
- Any important decisions should be taken to God. Be patient; the answers will come. Remember, it is in God's timing.
- At each AR meeting, write down the prayer requests. When the going gets tough, pray for them. This gets us out of ourselves.

Before bed

- Thank God for another day.
- Review our day, and ask God for His forgiveness where we have been wrong. Seek what we can do better.
- Ask God to help us love Him more.
- Ask God to help us love others more.

Night prayer: "God, forgive me where I have been resentful, selfish, dishonest, and afraid today. Show me what I can do better and where and how to take corrective measures. Help me not to keep anything to myself that may be troubling me but to discuss it openly with another person. Show me where I may owe amends, and grant me the courage to make it. Help me to be kind and loving toward others. Free me of worry and guilt that I may serve You better, my Lord. Amen."

Practice these basic fundamentals every day. Stay in God's word. Continue to fellowship with like-minded people. And when God puts something on your heart, share it with others. Always look toward the bigger picture. We work for God. Seek what His will is for us because He has a plan for our lives in the long run.

CHAPTER 6

Fellowship

Fellowship with other believers is vital in recovery, especially when we are new. We entered God's world when His spirit came into us. This gives us the right to be called children of God. We have a seed in us that needs nourishment if it is to grow and be planted in others. This requires that we learn more humility, discipline, and the strengthening of our faith. We do this by gathering together with other believers who are equally yoked.

Iron sharpens iron, as one man sharpens another. Without each other, they would become dull and useless. When believers come together with shared convictions, there is a real unity in Spirit. This is considered genuine biblical fellowship. We draw strength from other believers, especially those like us who have been cured of alcoholism. Faith comes from hearing and leads us to doing! We need to hear God's word as it is preached and taught. In it, we learn of His love for us and also how He wants us to live. If you are having trouble finding a group that practices these very principles, we encourage you to join us. In the back of this book, you will find information on how to get in touch with us.

Let us tell you about the AR fellowship. Most of us feel like when we meet, it's the highlight of our day. It's a place where we have found true friends and real companionship. We have family members and friends who attend also. We joke, we laugh, and sometimes cry. But believe us, it's always tears of joy. Many might be shocked at our levels of freedom and happiness, but why shouldn't we be? Each in our turn has been delivered out of a life of turmoil and experienced a miracle. We seldom talk about drinking problems in our meetings because we have none. We are no longer alcohol conscious; we are God conscious! You might ask, "What about the newcomer?" That's simple. When they want what we have, then they will do what we do. Until then, we prefer for them to just listen. Sometimes, selfishness and self-centeredness must be handled with tough love. After all, it's the saving of the soul that we of AR are concerned with. Sobriety is just one of the fruits of a changed life. There are much greater gifts, which we feel responsible for passing on.

When a newcomer joins, we believe in getting them into the cure right away. He or she is assigned a sponsor and other elders to counsel with them if they honestly mean business. Sometimes the alcoholic may have to do some more research on learning about their illness before they are willing to accept our way of living.

Unfortunately, there's only one way to find out. By no means do we want to rob the alcoholic of "the gift of desperation." It may be the only hope they ever have in coming to the knowledge of the truth!

God and the Bible hold the ultimate authority here in AR. We sometimes use other commentaries as well; however God and His word come first. Our meetings open with a prayer, followed by a witness, who brings a message on a topic from the Bible or another spiritual reading. He or she then shares their hope, healing, and recovery around that. Then we open the floor for feedback. We also conduct Bible studies and try to tie them into our recovery. It really works, especially for our spiritual growth and our relationship with our Father in heaven. We designate one night a week for someone to share their testimony/story. All of our meetings end in prayer. Also, we have a prayer chain, where we pray as a group for others who are in need. We have seen many prayers answered from cancer and other difficulties. Not only as individuals do we have a job to do, but as a group, our faith in prayer avails much!

What a blessing God Almighty has given us in this fellowship of the redeemed. What a great opportunity to love and be loved and be a part of this miracle of healing. We have the means of getting well, staying hopeful, and best of all, serving Him. God is great!

CHAPTER 7

Love and Service

God's greatest commandments are to love Him with all your heart and to love others as yourself. When we took the first four steps, we were reborn in Spirit. This enabled us to commune with God as outlined in step five. In it, we learned discipline, and we received the love of God and love for our fellow man. In step six, we learned the importance of fellowship. This taught us more humility and strengthened our faith. It also taught us how to get along with others and work together toward a common goal. This is putting on the armor of God as He prepares us for the task at hand.

Surrender, confession, restitution, and communion gave us a life-changing experience. Passing this on to others ensures that this experience grows. As redeemed alcoholics, our primary focus should be to serve God and pass this message on to others, especially other alcoholics who are still suffering. This is the will of God for us.

A fire was ignited the moment we experienced this miracle. Each of us couldn't wait to tell others what had happened in our lives. We learned a few hard lessons in doing this. We can't give away something we don't have.

Therefore, we must be sure of our relationship with God. We get this right first! This requires the absolute obliteration of self! There is no greater love given than when we deny ourselves so that others can live. But we must remember, no matter how bad we want it to happen for the next person, nothing happens unless God says so.

The outcome is not up to us. Our job is to deliver the message, not watered down either! The truth hurts sometimes, but it's the truth that sets us free.

There are people all around us that have never heard this news, such as family, neighbors, and friends. Some of these people may even know others suffering from the very illness we overcame. We should be ready to give an answer for the light that is in us at all times. There are really no set rules on how to do this. We learn as we go, and we've got to start somewhere. We become good witnesses by witnessing. Our own experience is our best asset. No one knows our story better than we do. This message should be spoken with tactical common sense. Be patient, knowing the testing of your deeds produces perfect faith.

Working with another alcoholic, who is still sick, is a whole other ball game in and of itself. We should know this. We all know what it took for us. The same should be considered when working with a new person. Most alcoholics don't know what it really means to be one. Having been there ourselves, we can share how we once struggled and get them to identify with us. Before proceeding into the remedy, explain to them the fatal nature of the disease. Tell them about the condition of the mind, known as an obsession. Show them how this compulsion causes them to drink against their will. Explain the allergy of the body and how once they start, they cannot stop. The more hopeless the new person feels, the better. The more his/her pride and ego are deflated, the more receptive they will be in accepting what we have to offer. In no way do we continue until the new person fully accepts their disease. We will be doing them an injustice if we do. We carry the message, not the alcoholic!

Well, this brings us to the final phase of our development, although there is nothing final about it! Practicing love and service should continue for our lifetime in all areas of our lives. One of our members said that the hardest thing he ever had to do was go back to work sober. He soon started becoming irritable toward his coworkers. He then started applying the principles of step five in this very situation. He soon found those ill feelings replaced by love. After continued prayer, our friend witnessed a change in his coworkers.

Some of them were even converted. What a gift we of Alcoholics Redeemed have been given, and a much bigger blessing than that is to be able to give this gift away to others.

> For God so loved the world, that he gave his
> only begotten Son, that whosoever believeth in
> him should not perish, but have everlasting life.
> (John 3:16 KJV)

May God bless you and keep you until then.

Testimonials

LIFE FROM A DUCK BLIND

I was born in a small town in California. My parents divorced when I was young, and I spent most of my childhood with my grandparents, aunt, and uncle. It was there that I learned to hunt and fish and also work hard. At nineteen years old, I decided to join the army. I immediately deployed to Somalia in the early nineties. What a culture shock that was. I remember thinking there can't be a God because He wouldn't let people live like this. Today, I can say "God is," and this is what happens when a country loses faith and morals. After completing my service to my country, my drinking began to get heavy at times. I had a lot of fun, and alcohol made me feel like the life of the party. It was then that I met my wife, and we had two sons. I told myself it was time to settle down and raise a family. It was then that I decided to quit drinking, not knowing the disaster that lay ahead. My thirtieth birthday was coming up, and my wife suggested we take the kids to the snow. We arrived at a cabin that her parents had rented, and surprising me, they were throwing a surprise birthday party. I was shocked. I didn't see it coming. My father-in-law handed me a can of beer. I didn't see that coming either. I took a drink, and I felt like I was on top of the world. I said, "Wow, do you have another?" Unfortunately, he only brought an eighteen pack. I drank everything he had and still craved more. Unfortunately, we were snowed in, and it was miserable. I soon learned that the only thing worse than not drinking was not getting enough once you start. This sparked a ten-year run for me. I began sneaking it and hiding it. My truck became the bar. My marriage started to fall apart, along with my job. I was restrained from seeing my boys and ended up alone. I soon lost everything worthwhile in life.

Sometime after the Fourth of July, in the year 2011, I was scrounging change just to get a cheap can of beer. As I stumbled in this alleyway, I had that magic moment in my life—total defeat. All at once, I couldn't go no further.

I was driven to a treatment center in Santa Rosa, California. I had been there before, but this time was different. I was willing to sacrifice anything to quit drinking forever. On July 9, 2011, I woke up in detox. And through God's grace, I haven't had a drink since. It was suggested to me to go into a sober living home. I did. I was also told to go to AA. I did. In AA, I was told, "Don't drink, no matter what, and go to ninety meetings in ninety days." I did. And did I get sicker and sicker? I did.

Then a miracle began to take shape. My aunt and uncle came to visit me. My aunt saw me desperate and crying. She asked, "What's wrong?"

I said, "I don't know." I told her how I was depressed and suicidal. She asked if I was going to my meetings and did I have a sponsor. I said, "Yes, but it all makes no sense. They keep saying the same things: Don't drink and go to meetings; get a higher power, and stay away from slippery places and slippery things. One guy even suggested I go down to the beach and get a rock and throw it as hard as I could and let it all go."

It was then that my aunt began to tell me a story about her dad. She said he was a true alcoholic and that he got sober in the 1950s in Texas. She described him as having an X factor to alcohol. She handed me his old book that she had kept all these years. The book was entitled *Alcoholics Anonymous* second edition. I began to read it and soon found out what was wrong with me. This was a crushing blow that snuffed out all my pride and ego that I could beat the game on my own. I suddenly needed and wanted God. He came. I surrendered my life entirely to Him. I faced my sins and humbled myself before the Lord, and He amazingly lifted me up. I began to make restitution to those I had harmed from my drinking. My life changed. I felt something new that I had never experienced before. Peace of mind began to take over. The thought came to me that there must be thousands of true alcoholics that don't understand their predicament. I commenced to tell others and share my testimony. A fellowship of men, women, family, and friends began to take shape. I'm so grateful to be a part of this miracle of healing. For all of these blessings, I thank Him, the One who presides over us all!

REDEEMED

I was fortunate to grow up in a home where I felt loved and valued by my parents. We went to church regularly. One summer, at our church camp, I invited Jesus into my life. I remember how different I felt. Even as a nine-year-old child, I felt His presence come into me. As the years passed though, I let this relationship become lukewarm. I continued to go through the motions of this relationship by going to church, being involved in ministries, marrying a Christian, taking our kids to church, yet all the while missing the mark.

Drinking wasn't a part of my life at this time. However, I do remember, at six years old, taking a sip of wine at a friend's house. I don't remember the first time I drank pop, milk, or coffee, but that memory is etched in my mind.

Several years ago, I experienced some life-altering events. The emotional pain was deep. One night, I went out with a girlfriend who knew what I was going through. She suggested that we have a glass of wine. I will never forget the wonderful feeling of comfort and relaxation. All the pain was numbed. It was amazing! I felt like, "Where have you been all my life!"

Over time I would drink more often. It became difficult to hide what I was doing from my husband. I had to sneak bottles in and out of the house and disguise my drinks. My hiding places became quite creative. My husband became a sleuth and would inevitably find them. My drinking was progressive. I would obsess over it and plan every event and free moments around it. I ruined family times and vacations away. I was unable to talk with my adult children on the phone in the evenings without detecting that I'd been drinking. I was no longer drinking to numb pain but was drinking to satisfy a craving beyond my control.

Many times, I woke up in fear and dread about what had happened the night before. It was torture to face my husband and his disdain for me. He would ask why I kept making such bad choices. I didn't know why. I would be genuinely remorseful and promise not to drink again. A day or two later, the memory of that would be replaced with thoughts of, *This time I'll control it*—one more attempt and one more failure.

One summer evening, we were going to an outdoor concert with friends. I started drinking in the afternoon and disguised my drink so I could continue to drink at the concert. The next morning, I woke up not remembering the concert or how the night had played out. My husband was so upset and proceeded to try to tell me details. I stopped him, too ashamed and embarrassed to hear about it. After he left the house, I knew what I needed to do. I couldn't imagine my life anymore with alcohol, but I couldn't imagine my life without it. My family would be better off without me, I believed. I tried to take my life. While in intensive care for three days, God came.

He surrounded me with a warm blanket of overwhelming love. He assured me that everything was going to be okay. I felt His presence, just like I had as a child at summer camp when I asked Jesus into my heart. It was a powerful and profound experience. God took away the obsession to drink!

This was the beginning of my new life in Christ. The AR steps helped me confess my sins and make amends for the harm I had done to others. It also helped me learn about my disease and the root of my problem. AR provided the place and the tools I needed to grow in my walk with Jesus. Since turning my life back over to Him, I have found peace in my life like I have never known. I no longer look to alcohol for ease and comfort. Christ is sufficient! He carries my problems as I walk in peace, no matter what is happening around me.

Today I believe that God made me an alcoholic for a reason. I am called to reach out to other alcoholics. Today I work for God. He puts people and situations in my path so I can be a vessel to help them realize they too can be cured from this deadly disease and experience a beautiful new life. God has turned the wreckage of my past into something useful for His purposes, and for this I am extremely grateful!

TIDAL WAVE

I am the youngest of three and grew up in beautiful British Columbia, Canada, in a music-filled Dutch Christian home. I had a safe and loving childhood, but I struggled a lot growing up. I had major anxiety and fear of abandonment, nightmares, tummy aches, and insecurity. We moved a lot, so I found myself being the new kid and having a hard time fitting in and adjusting. This caused instability and feelings of inferiority.

When I was thirteen, my relationship with alcohol started, which soon led to drugs, bad relationships, and my drinking career. The next twenty-five years, I made decisions based on my feelings, and that got me into quite a bit of trouble. Guilt, shame, worthlessness, and brokenness became my best buddies. Things would happen in life, and all I knew how to do was numb—numb the pain, numb the reality, numb the truth, numb the joy, numb the good, and numb the bad. After all, there was always a reason to lift a glass, either in celebration or in sadness. I became an expert at self-sabotage and ensured I would be the one to destroy everything good before anyone had the chance to do so for me.

I had a few key people in my life that were constant and were always trying to lead me to the Father by showing unconditional love and kindness and being true examples of Jesus. My dad was one of those. When cancer took him in 2008, it absolutely broke me. I was twenty-three. I had a husband, a house, a dog, a decent job, and on the outside, it seemed I had a good life. But I was utterly and hopelessly broken and in despair. Living a selfish and self-centered life, losing my dad was the ultimate abandonment. How could he have left me? How could God have done this? This helped me feel justified in my drinking, and things only got worse. I went to many lengths to try and "be happy." Nothing filled the hole. I had a brilliant idea of going on a two-year around-the-world trip, thinking once I found a certain place or saw a bunch of cool countries and cultures, I would find contentment. I would have freedom. It was like chasing that first high and never being able to reach that place again. Those years weren't all bad though. I have incredible memories and experiences that I'm very grateful for. Life was a party. As long as I had my bestie boozie with me, I was good. I had some extreme highs, met a lot of beautiful people, saw a lot, loved passionately, and did some pretty cool stuff. But none of it was enough. Everything had a time limit, and before I knew it, I would be back in my deep, dark hole. Satan had me right where he wanted me. I was at his mercy. Soon after that trip, I was divorced, had no home, no direction, no job, and really thought my life was over. I wanted to die but was too afraid to actually do it. I hit bottom hard this time. My beloved sister-in-law took me in yet again in an attempt to help me rebuild my life. She wanted me to be free more than I knew how. She modeled God's love and patience, His tenderness and mercy, but I couldn't receive it. I thought she was absolutely crazy for loving me so much. There was progress in my life, and I was able to face some brutal consequences and own some of my shortcomings, ask for forgiveness to some I had hurt, and taste a bit of freedom, grasp onto hope and God. But I couldn't give it all to Him, and I lacked true understanding of who He really is and certainly didn't know what Jesus dying on the cross for my sins meant. Somehow, I thought I was the special one that was exempt from what God gave us through His Son, Jesus Christ. I had this attitude that I needed to suffer for all the bad choices I made and also for my lack of control over the bottle. Freedom from all the bondage and chains became something I wanted so badly. Eventually, a life event would give me the excuse to drink again, but alcoholism is progressive, so although I would have periods of me without it, it was waiting for me when I picked it up again. I was too prideful and afraid to face the truth, so I continued to suffer silently inside.

I remarried, was blessed with three children, and loved with all my heart. I fought hard to attain peace, especially since I got a second chance at life. But I was still an alcoholic, so nothing worked. Not even for my beautiful children could I stop for. How pathetic I felt.

I finally hit rock bottom and succumbed to full surrender on October 14, 2022. I was so ready and willing to change my life because I knew, if I didn't, it would be death for me. A miracle took place when I completely gave my life to the Father. I let Him not only into my life for real but let Him take over, 100 percent full control. I faced my stuff. Accepting God's forgiveness was the greatest gift. Finally understanding God's great love for me and making the choice to forgive myself was the beginning of my true freedom. Taking full responsibility for my actions and making amends was a beautiful, humbling process. Letting go of resentments and anger were also crucial to my life change. Dying to myself and accepting the consequences for my actions has been more freeing than I ever thought possible. When I gave my life to God, He took away all of the brokenness, and the obsession with alcohol broke off as an added gift.

Finally, my tidal wave changed, and the waves started coming on shore with peace and joy, forgiveness and love, acceptance and humility, hope and a future—true redemption at last. God led me to Alcoholics Redeemed, and I have learned that all I had to do was surrender my life entirely to Him. He takes care of not only alcoholism but breaks bondage, fear, inadequacy, insecurity, and much more. By doing AR's steps and following a simple daily plan centered around guidance and obedience to God in all things, having a grateful heart in all circumstances, praying in everything, and having humility every day, I can truly say I am free. I have peace, am content, and live life in abundance! I have a life that I didn't even know was possible!

God has provided for my children and me every moment of every day. His blessings are endless. Now I can see it! Life is enjoyable in the moment, and there's no constant pull taking me back to the past or even forward to the future. God is the good shepherd, and I am His sheep. He is so kind. He is gentle and patient. He has a great plan for my life and has given me so much hope. He has changed the desires of my heart to please Him and do His work. My mission is to spread His love and help other alcoholics who think there is no way out.

RESTORATION THROUGH DESPERATION

Not everyone's story involves complete destruction, but we all reached a point of desperation. My childhood wasn't a bad one at all. I had loving parents, three great siblings, and was raised in a Christian household. I have always been active in church life. But along my journey, I have wrestled between worship of myself and of God.

I was always really close to my brother. From the outside, people never saw the similarities between either of us. He was lean, dark haired, and similar to the prodigal son, while I was stout, light haired, and the übernerd. While we were quite different, we always had each other's back.

Our first major bonding session involved a bottle of bourbon. I remember two things that night: I could play Contra on Nintendo for hours, and bourbon took me to my knees faster than anything I ever had.

During high school and college, I was a hard drinker, but it was usually contained to the weekends. As I saw it, I could party hard because I did what was sought of me. I had a good job; I was a home-owner; and I led church youth ministries. However, in my twenties, I started getting annoyed with my church, and I began to live more in the world. It was during this time I was married and had two daughters. My drinking was always there but was never seen as problematic. It was, however, always one of excess. It only took some life events to flip my will over to the bottle. A highly stressful job, multiple kids, diverging goals with my wife, and constant travel started the recipe of disaster. Then the oven began cooking in 2018, when I would hit two of the most devastating things in my life. On Easter, my brother died at the age of thirty-six from a fentanyl overdose. I remember his cold body, and after, that I began drinking heavily. That started a steady binge that continued for two years.

About two months after my brother died, my third daughter was born two and a half months premature. She was essentially raised in an incubation unit, and it was a chore for my wife and me to see her. It created a host of resentments between my wife and me that lasted until my sobriety.

I began to drink more and more. Everything I worked for seemed meaningless. The house, the wife, the family, and the career didn't make me happy. I spent the greater part of the next two years seeking isolation, drinking heavily at nights, and growing further into depression. Eventually, in 2020, I realized I couldn't continue as things were and left my job.

While I had another job lined up, I didn't expect COVID lockdowns, and my best-laid plans fell through on me. I couldn't find work; my wife and I fought constantly; and I drank more and more. Despite dropping forty pounds from lower stress, my anger and drinking eventually lead my wife to stay with her parents. I eventually went through a two-week depression that would have been booze intensive, but I wasn't able to hold anything down.

In the following weeks, I admitted to myself I had a problem. I felt hopeless. I tried what everyone suggested, and nothing worked. In that time, I decided to go to AA. The initial weeks were great. I met a sponsor, and I started doing the steps. It wasn't until I really did step one that my eyes were truly opened. I will always thank my AA sponsor and the steps for pushing me to let go. But just like my resentments, I also had to let AA go as well. My sponsor introduced me to Alcoholics Redeemed, and the rest became history.

Recovery comes from God alone and a healthy spiritual relationship with Him. There is no other way. I found that God helped me release many things holding me back. I found purpose with Him. In fulfilling Christ's two commandments in Matthew 24:36–40, which are to love God with your whole heart and to love others as yourself, I started seeing life through a new lens. I found meaning as I walked others to the same freedom I have in Christ.

I hope, if you are reading this testimony, you've reached the moment of desperation where you too can find the same freedom and purpose that we have found.

NOTHING CHANGES IF NOTHING CHANGES

I loved my dad very much. However, love is not enough to stop any true alcoholic from drinking. My dad was a career military man and served during World War II, where he married my mom, and later, they had my sister and me. We lived with my dad drinking for many years. We were too embarrassed to have any friends over, and my mom hardly left the house. Not knowing why my dad drank made it even harder. We were stationed in Oklahoma when I was ten years old, and my sister was seven. The drinking and fighting became so bad that it caused my mom to have a nervous breakdown. She was hospitalized, and my sister and I were sent to live with my dad's brother in South Dakota. We stayed there for eighth months, where we were introduced to cold weather, farm life, and a new school. Eventually, we were reunited with my mom when she was released from the hospital, and we were sure that Dad wouldn't be drinking after this.

However, that was not the case.

My dad soon got transferred to Abilene, Texas, and our whole family moved again. His drinking progressed for the worst, causing me to feel bitterness, worry, frustration, and hopelessness. After being in Abilene for two years, my dad was caught drinking while his unit was on alert. This was a major violation that almost ended his military career. However, it turned out to be the best thing that could ever happen to my dad and us.

Whether my dad found AA or AA found him, I will never know. Today I truly know that the Lord works in mysterious ways. On April 19, 1959, my dad surrendered his life to God and took the necessary steps. He never touched another drop up until his death in 1989. This miracle was to change our whole family's lives forever. There were AA family groups in those days. We all went together, and we were required to take the steps as well. One of the most freeing moments is when I made amends to my dad for the resentments that I had toward him. I'll never forget it.

When my dad was two years sober, we got stationed at Castle AFB in Atwater, California, where my dad would eventually retire. My dad continued on with the program, helping others with the same illness. He gave every moment of his life to his family and gave back to what was so freely given to him. He was a genuine, caring, and loving man right up until he passed away just after his thirtieth anniversary of sobriety.

As for me, I went on to pursue my calling in church ministry, working with youth and children for about twenty years. I have been married to my wonderful husband for just over fifty-eight years now. We have one daughter. I am forever grateful for the blessings God has given me and my family.

In 2011, my nephew's life fell apart due to his drinking. I was able to give him my dad's old big book that I had saved. He found the same thing that my dad found, and I got to witness yet another miracle. When COVID hit in 2020, we were no longer able to go to church, and my nephew couldn't attend his meetings either. After continued prayer on both sides, another miracle of healing began to take shape. God gave my nephew a vision of a new approach to alcoholism. A program of redemption was born in which we all get to participate online. I got to start a women's group, using my experience with church and alcoholism as a child. I'm so fortunate that I get to pass this message on to others all over the world. Sometimes our lives have to be completely shaken up, changed and rearranged in order to relocate us to the place where we are really meant to be.

RADICAL REDEMPTION

I went to church periodically as a child. Much of it is a blur to me. I never really understood the whole salvation plan back then. At the age of eight, I was diagnosed with type 1 diabetes. This rocked my family's world. It was at this point where I felt completely different from my peers. I had no idea that deep inside me was a disease that lingered and wanted me to be dead.

Alcohol was introduced to me at the age of fifteen. It made me feel normal and connected to others. I had no idea that participating in this lifestyle, which at the time seemed typical to me, had the potential to kill me. Drinking alcohol as a type 1 diabetic can cause adverse effects, even death. God's radical love and grace would protect me for many years to come. Not only was I drinking, but I also was engaging in adulterous actions, seeking whoever and whatever to make me feel good. Whether it was drinking, drugs, or sex, these became the norm for me.

At the age of twenty-two, I was invited to go to a church revival by my neighbor. This short, brief interval kept me from drinking and partying temporarily. This is where the vicious disease, the obsession of the mind, kept trying to get me. I was obsessed over it. My thoughts during this time were, *Surely, I can have a drink. Surely, it couldn't hurt anything or anyone.*

At this time, I was diagnosed with diabetic retinopathy. The church family gathered around and supported me. I am forever grateful for those relationships to this day. It was nine months later that I left the church. What followed was the full-blown self-will to do all that I was obsessing over. This soon would come to a screeching halt by a divine intervention.

On July 6, 1990, while in a dark barroom, I heard a voice that said, "This is not the plan I have for you. This is not who I made you to be. You have a child at home that needs you." This scared the living daylights out of me. I had never had this type of experience before. I went home, got down on my knees, and cried out, "God, if that was You, I am going to need Your help to stop drinking." God did just that. He sent me, through a friend, to AA. I heard the explanation of my condition, that I had a disease, an obsession of the mind, followed by an allergic reaction of the body, and that there was a cure. That cure was God and that I could seek and find Him. After five years of AA, soberness just did not seem to be enough. I knew there must be more. God's radical intervention came again.

I was invited to go back to that same church, and I said *yes*. Three years in, I went to a healing service. I had no idea what that was. This is where God healed my eyes from complete blindness that I had from the side effects of drinking and unmanaged diabetes. I am alive today because of His great love, grace, protection, and restoration.

Shortly after Alcoholics Redeemed began in 2020, a friend invited me to attend one of their meetings. This is where I found the connection with like-minded believers, who had also struggled with alcoholism. This is what God says in His word, "Who redeems your life from destruction, who crowns you with loving kindness and tender mercies" (Psalm 103:4 NKJV).

I was once a hopeless drunk and now a redeemed child of God. It is because of His mercy that I am sharing His story of radical redemption.

LAST CALL

I had twenty-four years of continuous sobriety. On my fiftieth birthday, the insanity of the first drink reared its ugly head. The thought that I could have one drink came to mind. Before I knew it, I was off and running. This goes to show that sobriety alone is not enough for a true alcoholic. Alcoholism took me to a dark place. It destroyed my family, relationships, career, my health, wealth, and self. Each day, my only thought was to be sure that I had enough alcohol to get through the day. The sickness and the pain without it were too much to bear. The loss and hurt I incurred and caused my family and all who cared about me were so incredibly heartbreaking.

Several treatment centers later, without success, I was at a loss and felt doomed to an alcoholic death. I could not fathom life with alcohol or without it. I have never felt so desperate in my life. I believed that I needed to be locked up, regulated, supervised, scrutinized, and babysat to be free from alcohol.

Then God sent me what I call an angel. I met a lady in the rooms of AA that shared in meetings. She stood out to me. There was something about her. I wanted what she had. We became friends, and she sent me daily devotionals. However, I didn't read them and ended up in detox yet again. She told me about this new program called Alcoholics Redeemed. It was in this detox center that I attended my very first meeting. I will never forget the welcome I received from everyone at that meeting. I was taken back. I had never been welcomed anywhere like this. I was told that the group had been praying for me for several months. This left me breathless and in tears. It moved me to the very core of my being. After the meeting, I felt like I had finally found a way out for the first time in eight years. I was so excited and couldn't wait to attend again.

Returning home from detox, I was taken through the steps of Alcoholics Redeemed. I surrendered the depths of my being to Christ Jesus. I knew I was doomed to an alcoholic death if I didn't. Like it is said, "the pain of the problem must be greater than the pain of the solution!" I was fully willing and open to the dying of my flesh. I confessed my faults and humbly asked God to cleanse me from all unrighteousness. The peace and joy that came over me that day was indescribable. I had never experienced this before. I was elated and excited in a way I never knew was possible. This glorious peace and joy has never left me since that day. I continued with the rest of the steps. I made amends to the people, places, and institutions that were harmed by my actions. I met with my sponsor once a week, and I attended meetings daily. I wanted to know God more and what His will was for me. I had never read the Bible or even been a part of any church through the fifty-seven years of my life. The guidance of the group members helped clarify so much of what I did not understand in the Bible. God's word has intrigued me to continue learning, trusting, and seeking His glorious ways. I faithfully commune daily with God, asking for His direction and His continued molding of me into the likeness of His glorious Son, Jesus Christ, my Lord and Savior.

I have been counseled throughout my life by psychologists and psychiatrists. They meant well, but it has been through Christ that I have truly found rest. Today I am completely free of the demise of alcoholism and have no desire to remain anywhere in my past. My heart's true desire is to remain humbly in God's strength and victory in all my weaknesses. With that said, everything inside of me has and is continuing to be renewed in Christ daily. It's been an experience of immeasurable abundance of love, forgiveness, protection, consistency, grace, mercy, and a heart full of worship. Praise to God for these blessings.

ME, MYSELF, AND MY SHADOW

Survival was the name of the game—New York City, Spanish Harlem, walking to school, watching my back, the bullying, drugs, and gang activities that surrounded me, not to mention my dad, who worked three jobs to support his family. I understand firsthand the emotional struggles that come with it, living in the memories of childhood sexual abuse, distrust, and low self-esteem.

What is my purpose? This is a question that I often asked myself. Trying to fit into society and comparing myself to others left me with feelings of inadequacy. I created this false idea that I am not enough and not as intelligent or productive as others. I was alive but not living.

As a single mother of three, I felt overwhelmed with caring for my children and working full-time to support us. I also had to care for my parents when they became ill, and I thought I had lost my identity and was living my life to care for everyone else. This led to alcoholism. I would refer to myself as a functioning alcoholic, but was I functioning? I was robotically doing everything society expected of me, but I was absent. I struggled with relationships and found comfort in isolation. I could drink all I wanted when no one was watching; I didn't have to take the bottle out of hiding. I felt shame, but I couldn't stop.

I remember the day I took my first sip; I was about thirteen. I wouldn't say I liked the taste, but it did something for me. Soon alcohol became my shadow. If I wasn't drinking it, I was thinking about it and always chasing the buzz. In 2008, for the first time, I experienced death. I lost my father to cancer, and six months later, my fiancé to a heart attack, both of whom were heavy drinkers. I had thought I was already struggling with my shadow, but I had not experienced anything yet. I now began to medicate that horrible feeling of loss and abandonment with more alcohol. I didn't want to be at home, and I didn't want to be in company. I'd go out to bars and clubs by myself and would watch people while I drank, then I would go home and drink some more.

I remember the day one of my coworkers asked me to join her for a drink. I jumped at the opportunity. Little did I know that on that day, I would be meeting someone I would be with for the next twelve years. He was perfect for me. We had something in common: He liked to drink, and I didn't have to pretend. Quickly, I became an even heavier drinker than I was, but I had company now. The relationship took a toll on me. The verbal and mental abuse was overbearing, but my obsession with alcohol had already stolen my self-worth. I couldn't live with it, and I couldn't live without it. Not only had alcohol taken over my mind, but it was also taking my health.

In 2011, one morning after a night of binge drinking, while driving to work, I began to experience bad pain in my chest, soon to find out I had just experienced a mild heart attack, but even that experience was not enough to scare me sober. My health continued to deteriorate as the years went by. My self-esteem was so low. And while I wanted to get myself out of that toxic relationship, I could not build the courage to run away.

I was back in the hospital and needed to undergo major surgery. No one came to see me. The loneliness and hurt I felt was indescribable. I went home from surgery, and I had not learned my lesson. I prayed to God to heal me from this horrible disease, but I would serve myself a drink shortly after. I often said I'd stop tomorrow but couldn't do it. I liked it too much, how it made me feel, and how it helped me numb the feelings I had created.

In 2022, I hit bottom. It was the day I wholeheartedly cried out to God, and He showed me a clear picture of my life if I did not surrender to His will. God led me to Alcoholics Redeemed. I met many people who had once suffered from this same disease, saw something different in them, and wanted what they had. The fellowship was unlike anything I had ever experienced. It was a true brotherhood. Their focus was on God and not just on getting sober. It was then that I allowed God to work in me. Together we were learning how to put God first in our lives. I began to seek God in every circumstance, and it was then that I began to feel a life-changing transformation. My family, friends, and coworkers started to comment, "Whatever it is that you are doing, keep doing it! You are so different!" Some knew I had a problem, and others did not, but they could see a change in me.

God promised in Genesis 3:15 that even in our suffering, we would have victory, and I can testify to that. The steps in AR showed me a new way of living. The first thing I do in the mornings when I awake, I thank God and ask Him to guide me through the day. I am in constant connection with God in my decision-making. More importantly, I get to serve Him and help others, and I continuously seek the opportunity to share what God has done for me. Today I am flourishing as I actively seek God and pursue what He leads me to do. I no longer ask myself what my purpose is.

HE MADE THE WAY

Growing up the eldest of four, my childhood was always full, exciting, and fun. I had loving parents, who gave me every opportunity to succeed in life. There was no reason to believe what would come to pass. I found great enjoyment in sports, and my earliest memories were of feeling completely comfortable out on the sporting field. However, I felt extremely uncomfortable when the game had finished, and I found myself in social situations. I don't know where it comes from, but there was a sense of never fitting in. You could say it was like trying to it a square peg into a round hole. It was almost like everyone around me had the script sent to them at the start of the day, and it looked easy. But for me, I missed it and was scrambling. As I grew up, this was a trap I would continually fall into. I would compare myself to others and ask myself what was wrong with me. Little did I know at the time that this extremely self-centered view of the world would distort my way of life for years to come.

I resisted the first drink for some time as I saw my school friends getting drunk and their sporting performance decline. I told myself I was strong-willed and wanted to perform at the highest level, and I wasn't going to let anything get in my way. However, the inevitable day came when I took my first drink, and it changed everything! It lit me up like never before and instantly changed my perception of reality. Life had gone from black and white to a world of color. As the warmth of a drink filled me up, I found I could finally be comfortable in my own skin. At last, I could be me.

As the fears and insecurities melted away, people I felt so awkward to be around became my best friends. I could talk and laugh and not have a worry in the world about what anyone thought of me. After being on the outside for so long, I was suddenly in the middle, and I loved it. I was ten feet tall and bulletproof, invincible, and the world was mine.

My relationship with alcohol was truly love at first sight. I did not ease my way into it. Drinking became my priority, and everything else faded into the background. My only concern was where the next party was. It did something for me that it seemingly wasn't doing for others. They had the ability to stop if things were getting out of control. They could call it a night because they had to work the next day. For me, as soon as alcohol hit my lips, all bets were off, and there was no knowing when I would stop and where I would end up. It had me in its grips, and the delusion I lived in was that I was in control. The next drink became my master, and everything I did revolved around it, no matter what the consequences. Family and friends were eagerly awaiting the day I would grow up and start getting on with my life. That day did not come.

Those around me started to slow down the drinking and focus on education, careers, and starting families. My drinking took on more serious measures, and it was no longer a party. I had crossed that line. I'm not sure when it happened, but I was no longer bragging about my drinking. Instead, I started to hide it and drink in isolation. I was no longer with friends, chasing girls, and dancing all night. I was drinking to oblivion. I started to get involved with other substances, and I was regularly going out for days on end, where no one knew where I was. It was no longer waking up in bed with a hangover and talking about good times. Instead, it was going into blackouts and coming to hospitals, handcuffs, car crashes, and a multitude of frightening, life-threatening situations. At times I would seek medical help. And being heavily medicated, I would be counting sober days. Being sober felt like a prison sentence. I was continually going on the wagon, time to get it and healthy again or a new job or study or new friends or a new place to live. I always had a new plan and always found myself flat on my back again. This painful and agonizing cycle went on for years. I was in a war and did not even know it.

Something had to change. I could not imagine life with or without alcohol, and I wanted to die. There were many sad attempts to take my life, as I could not see a way out. I was physically, mentally, and emotionally wrecked. I had no idea I was also spiritually dead. Sad and depressed drunken sprees were the regular, where I would end up in a ball of tears, wondering how I ended up so lost. Alcohol had beaten me! I was a broken man. And in a lucid moment, I asked for help.

I was directed to rehabilitation centers and different programs. There was slight progress, but there was no peace in my sobriety. I had a lot of confusion and frustration, making up gods of my own understanding, and getting misguided from some well-meaning people. I was stuck in recovery circles. I would get sober; however, nothing had really changed in my life, and I was still doing a lot of the old behaviors. I felt like a phony, and I could no longer fake it. I reached a point of sober where I was going to drink or make the ultimate sacrifice. In absolute desperation, I cried out to God. In that precise moment, which I will never forget, He came. Something had changed. I could not articulate it at that moment, but it was like coming home. I had a deep sense that it was going to be okay. The thoughts of drinking or even harming myself vanished. What was to follow was nothing less than the miraculous hand of God.

The pandemic hit, and recovery meetings went online. The gold I had struck was not acceptable in these meetings. Higher power, god of your own understanding, or basically whatever you want to do was more of the liking. When I said that the Lord had delivered me from drinking, it would be frowned upon. It caused me to fall back into people-pleasing by saying the usual recovery language. I would be compliant in a meeting, but there was defiance within me, knowing this was not the truth. I became frustrated and angry. Once again, I cried out to the Father for help.

He led me to Alcoholics Redeemed. I was refreshed from my very first meeting when I heard, "This is not a sobriety program. This is a life-changing program." I sensed what God had led me to was very special and was filled with the Holy Spirit. I instantly wanted what they had, and I had a hunger that I had never experienced before. I was also comforted and reassured that they were talking about the One true God, and the only way to enter into that relationship is through His Son, Jesus Christ.

I was no stranger to "step work," and I almost sighed when my soon-to-be sponsor asked if we could meet. However, I was pleased with what took place. We were not going to spend months and months working on myself so I could stay sober yet another day. Instead, we were going to enter into a relationship with God, and I would be set free at last. It became obvious that even though I had a spiritual experience, I was not walking in victory. I was still stuck in strongholds and bondages, which kept me blocked. I could say I was a believer and saved or even go to church, but I did not have the freedom. Once this miracle took place from following AR's simple program, I have never looked back.

My life today is unrecognizable. It's no longer putting up an appearance concerned about the bank balance, job title, or the car I drive. It's about seeking God and being in His presence. As strange as it may sound, I would not have had it any other way. I will be forever grateful for everyone who tried to help me, but no human power could have saved me.

I no longer have to pretend and fake it to please other people. I was constantly in a world where I was so self-conscious and concerned about what others thought of me. It was exhausting! Today I know perfectly who I am in Christ. The freedom, peace, and joy that this brings is indescribable. I thought being an alcoholic was the worst thing that could have happened to me, turns out, it was a gift that led me to divine help and a relationship with God. Today I am filled with gratitude and thanksgiving as I've been given a life I do not deserve. I live a life beyond my wildest dreams. I am alive, justified, and redeemed!

A TEACHER'S NIGHTMARE

I was a married mother of four young children, a teacher, and a respected community member when things started to come undone. My husband got really sick, leaving me with most of the responsibility of raising the kids and managing the household. I was working to provide for everyone and maintain as much normalcy as possible. Not to mention the freezing cold temperatures and shoveling snow here in Alberta. It was overwhelming on a good day!

I had always been a drinker. I enjoyed cocktails with friends and overindulged myself from time to time on special occasions. After a long illness and subsequent transplant, my husband recovered and then left me. "You were too controlling," he said. Although in my mind, who else was there to manage the children, run the home, and coordinate the multitude of things that needed to happen each day? As the stress piled up, so did the empty wine bottles. I justified my drinking by saying, "You'd drink too if you were me." Alcohol paired well with everything, celebrating or commiserating, and it became an obsession that soon ran my life.

Then, to make matters worse, one of my children got very ill and was rushed to the hospital. As she clung to life in the ICU, I never left her side. I then had to learn how to care for a diabetic child. It was all too much. I began to rely on self-help books, hastily given advice from friends and family, and lots of alcohol to cope. My life began to spiral down. I made plans to fix myself, to quit drinking, and to be happy. I felt so alone in the chaos of guilt, shame, and sadness. I knew my children deserved better and that, ultimately, I deserved more. However, determined as I was, I couldn't get there on my own. I believed that if I didn't control everything, it would fall apart. That was exactly what happened, on my watch, with me running the show.

In the end, I was drinking in excess daily and couldn't remember many of the things I did or said or missed. My life was out of control, and it became torture trying to fix it alone. My parents came to my rescue and took the children to their father's house. I had found a recovery home on the internet. When I called the director, I asked her if there was a lot of religion in the program because I wasn't a religious person. She replied, "Only as much as you want there to be."

Once there, I spent time learning about the Bible and sharing stories with women I would have never thought I had so much in common with. As I was leaving the recovery house, a pastor recommended an online group called Alcoholics Redeemed and that became the beginning of my real walk with Jesus. I made the decision to turn my life over to God and to accept Christ as my savior. My life changed, and I began to experience peace I had never known.

It's amazing what the Lord can do when you let Him. With teenagers in the house now, life is anything but calm and predictable, but I never have to face challenges alone. The obsession to drink is long gone, but more importantly, I have faith that I am exactly where I'm supposed to be. I'm learning what God wants to teach me through these struggles, and I'm present in the moments that make life so worth living. I thank God every day for never giving up on me, even though I wasn't looking for Him back then. Today, I have gratitude in my heart for this life that is so much better than I could have planned.

INDEPENDENCE DAY

I'll never forget the summer between seventh and eighth grade. My best friend and I decided to check out his parents' liquor cabinet. We started out by opening the different bottles and just taking a sniff of what was inside. I remember the slight feeling of nausea brought on by having smelled the liquor. Did we dare taste it? We dared, just a small sip of this one, then that. My buddy told me to try a certain one that tasted so disgusting. I tried them all. We weren't doing it to get drunk; we didn't even know what that was all about. We just wanted to explore what we witnessed the adults doing, knowing it was forbidden for us children. We found out soon enough. I remember placing the bottles back in the cabinet just like they were arranged before so as not to cause any suspicion. I remember his mother coming home from the grocery store and helping her unload the groceries while trying to stay steady, walking to and from the car. I remember having a feeling like I'd never had in my life. All of a sudden, I had confidence and wasn't a shy little kid anymore. We joked and laughed at ourselves, staggering around. All was well in my little world for once. I finally found the way I could fit in.

I might have been an alcoholic teenager if it weren't for the distraction of sports. I was dedicated to being a top football player and did achieve this ambition at the high school level. I was a good student, and by the end of high school, I was offered multiple scholarships for both football and track. I accepted none of them and instead joined the marine corps. I wish I could say I made that decision because of a sincere desire to serve my country. Although this was true to some extent, it was really for a girl. I wanted to marry my high school sweetheart, something that going off to college wouldn't allow me to accomplish. I was also afraid of failure. I was afraid

I would fail in college, afraid I would fail as an athlete, afraid my young relationship would fail. If I became a marine, I would be a part of the best fighting force in the world, and no one would suspect my real fears of failure. So that's what I did.

After being promoted to the rank of sergeant and receiving an honorable discharge, I started a promising job with a company back home and flourished. I soon found myself among the ranks of corporate middle management. I felt I was on my way to conquering the world. This is where my drinking started to show signs of being problematic. I remember having to stay after hours to close the books each month and sneaking in a few beers when no one was around. I might have been fired for this, but the risk didn't stop me. During this time, I started a small home business on the side that kept me up late at night working on the computer. This gave me ample opportunity to drink every night without anyone knowing. I preferred drinking alone because I was ashamed about how much I consumed. Some guys bragged about being able to hold their liquor, and I remember a time when I did the same. I was well past those times and didn't want anyone to find out.

My first marriage ended in divorce. This allowed me to drink as much as I wanted out in the open with no fear of judgment or ridicule. I married again and didn't make much of an effort to hide my drinking from my new bride. In the great recession of 2008, the company I worked for closed its doors. I was now facing the reality that I hadn't conquered anything. I felt like I was failing at life, and the fears I had years ago were coming true. My first marriage had failed, and now I had no way to provide for my new wife and my two young children.

I decided to go into business with two of my former coworkers. One of my business partners showed up on a Saturday morning with an eighteen pack of beer. All of a sudden, those fears of failure vanished. I can drink now with impunity, no risk of being fired, no constraints of time. Maybe I would conquer the world after all.

For years I made up excuse after excuse to drink during the day: "It helps me with customer service," "our customers like a place to unwind with a cold beer or two when they are done for the day," and so on. It turned out that they certainly did like to unwind with a drink, and I was the perfect host, always a cold one in the fridge when they came by. Of course, I would have a few too. Before I knew it, I was constantly drunk. I was drinking from morning till night. I would cherish the time all the customers would leave so I could drink alone after hours away from any protest or disapproving looks. This was my life day in and day out. I knew it was destroying my marriage, my family, and my life, but I couldn't stop. Every night I swore to myself that tomorrow would be different, and I wouldn't drink. However, every night I found myself doing the same thing with no explanation.

My last night of drinking was July 4, 2019. I was home alone all day. By this time, my wife had left me and was staying with her parents. I remember working all day in the yard, trying to get the house ready to sell because I wouldn't be able to afford it on my own. Divorce was looming on the horizon. I was feeling more sorry for myself than usual because it was Independence Day, and I was alone. I decided to head out to the office to work on some much overdue paperwork. In reality, I just didn't want to sit at home all alone. It reminded me of how bad I had failed at life. There was cold beer in the fridge at the office. As always, I indulged. Knowing the cops would be out looking for drunk drivers, I decided to stop with the beer and sober up with some Gatorade and water. I gave it a good couple of hours before leaving for home. On the way home, I was pulled over. I wasn't even worried because I stopped drinking hours ago. While going through the sobriety test, I was thinking I could do this much better if I had a couple of drinks. I finally had the opportunity to blow in the breathalyzer and clear this whole thing up. I wanted to get home to my refrigerator full of beer. However, I blew over the limit. How could that be? There had to be something wrong with the machine!

The officer told me that if I knew of anyone who could pick me up, it would save me a night in jail. I called anyone I could think of that might actually be sober that night. I ended up getting a hold of my seventeen-year-old daughter, who arranged for her stepdad and boyfriend to come and get me. It's a humiliating experience to listen to the police turning you over to the custody of another man, let alone your ex-wife's husband. But either way, I was on my way home to my fridge. That was the last time alcohol had passed my lips and the first time I earnestly prayed to God for help.

They say hindsight is twenty-twenty, and that is all too true. It took me a while to realize that God answered my prayer the next morning. The answer seemed so simple but at the same time very complex. The first thought in my mind upon waking up was that I can never drink again. That was the answer. I had no idea how I was going to accomplish this feat, but I knew it had to happen. I decided I better find some help and ended up at a men's only AA meeting being held at a church. I have no idea what was talked about during this meeting except that I left feeling relieved that there are people like me in the world, and they seem to have beaten this thing, so I probably could too.

After a couple of weeks, I called a man, whom I had met at a meeting, and asked him to help me. He helped me understand what my problem was and how it could be solved. We worked the steps differently than how I was hearing it done in the meetings by other members. He didn't give me a call schedule to check in with him each day. I didn't have to write pages and pages about my feelings. He was kind but at the same time didn't pull any punches. He told me, if I wasn't ready to change my life forever, then I might as well head to the liquor store and keep drinking until I was. I recoiled at the thought. I was ready!

I remember giving myself to God on his living room floor. We got on our knees and prayed together. I remember leaving his house afterward with a feeling of relief. I knew I was on the way to a lifetime of sobriety. I no longer felt alone. I began to seek out those I had wronged, and I made restitution. This was an integral part in my recovery as an alcoholic and as a child of God. My life now consists of seeking His will constantly by studying His word, fellowshipping with other believers, and trying to help others.

Every Independence Day, I recognize another year of sobriety. It's not really about sobriety though. Like my sponsor always says, "I was sober every time before I got drunk." It's about a new life, a new creation. Today, I enjoy a new dependence on God and doing His will.